MW01290774

Taking Back October

For Believers in Pursuit of Godly Fun
by Beth Vice

*Do not be overcome by evil,
but overcome evil with good
Ro. 12:21
Beth Vice*

All Scripture quotations, unless otherwise noted, are
taken from the
HOLY BIBLE NEW INTERNATIONAL VERSION.

Front and back cover photos by Tara Newman, @
Selaphotography
http://www.selaphotography.com

In loving memory of Pastor Ralph Marchbanks, who spoke the Word with love and passion.
He had the courage to show the movie that opened my eyes and changed my life.

Table of Contents

Chapter One:
Fall, a Season of Fear?

I love the fall; it is second only to spring in my heart. This transition into winter, with splashes of color everywhere, makes me lift my head and savor every breath of the season. The air is thick with the scent of flowers warmed by the sun, leaves wet from dew. Birds, squirrels, and bees busily gather the last bounty of summer.   As the daylight hours grow shorter, all creation exerts itself to prepare for the changing weather.

Where we live, summer doesn't usually kick in until July. The best days are often in September and even October. It cools down at night; leaves turn gold, burgundy, orange, and rust. However, gardens are at their peak and the ocean breeze is milder than in June. The daylight lingers and the sun's rich and mellow rays invite me outside - for a walk, to putter in the yard, to eat lunch or read on our deck.

I have happy memories of fall. My family's yearly trip to Clear Lake is a favorite. We packed a lunch and piled into the car, full of anticipation. My sisters, Mom, and I leaned over to admire the underwater world, as Dad rowed our rented skiff across the lake. Even though it averages 526 feet deep, fish, logs, plants and rocks all seemed just within reach in the shimmering water. Flaming deciduous trees on the hills cast a twin reflection in the water.

My parents delighted us girls with talk of leaf crunching, as if it were a forbidden pleasure. At the park, our backyard, or crossing the church parking lot, we gleefully crunched our way through crisp leaves, swishing them into the air to watch them float back down. The tradition continued with my own girls, and now my husband and grandchildren.

I still love fall. However, with frightening ferocity, the season God created for harvest and His magnificent color display, has become an all-out horror show. I walk the neighborhood and notice bushes and doorways swathed in cobwebs, as if abandoned long ago. Bodies are strewn about; a skeleton hangs from a nearby tree; tombstones dot the lawn. Driving through town at night, there's an eerie glow of orange from strings of lights. Pumpkins grin fiendishly from windows and porches. I feel the darkness. This is the face of October in America.

Americans spent $7 billion on Halloween in 2013, ranking second only to Christmas. An online article on "MSN Money" by Jim Probasco details some scary facts about the increasing amount of sales:

"Overall, consumer spending on 'all things Halloween' has increased a whopping 54.7 percent since 2005 making it a significant source of retail revenue...$2.6 billion on costumes...$330 million on costumes for their pets...more than $2 billion [for candy]. Halloween greeting cards will cost an additional $360 million...almost $2 billion on decorations, including skeletons, spider webs, inflatable Frankenstein monsters, and various other ghoulish yard and interior paraphernalia."

http://money.msn.com/investing/post--americans-will-spend-nearly-dollar7-billion-on-halloween

Further in the article, Probasco mentions the increasingly macabre products offered by major companies such as Sears, Wal-Mart, and Amazon. All three carried an item called the "Dead Dog" for online shoppers. Shocked by the photo and description, buyers complained on company Facebook pages. The product was immediately taken off the market.

If those *looking* for ways to turn their homes into haunted houses are disturbed by how sinister

Halloween products have become, what do the people of God have to say on this subject? I'm encouraged by the increasing number of families and churches choosing to turn away from this non-Christian holiday, but most still participate in festivities which have nothing to do with Christianity.

Chapter Two: Copying the World

It was potluck movie night and a couple in our Sunday school class volunteered to host the gathering. I arrived excited for an evening of fun and fellowship...until I entered their home. I looked for a place to put my jacket and purse in the entryway. Every surface was decorated for Halloween: cottony cobwebs, a light up jack-o-lantern and skull, and a bowl of black and orange candy. A resin witch figure stood nearby and cackled a "welcome."

With a sense of dread, I took my plate of goodies to the dining room and set it on the white tablecloth. It was trimmed with streamers of black cats, the tabletop dotted with ghosts, and Halloween dishes laden with food. My stomach lurched.

It's one thing to be greeted with such Halloween enthusiasm in the secular world. Stores, banks, restaurants, even doctor and dentist's offices go all out these days. They advertise ghoulish wares and employees exert themselves to "join in the fun." I wonder how fun it feels to small children who find themselves face to face with frightening images right at their eye level - figurines of witches, ghosts, and monsters that burst into fiendish laughter or haunting moans as they pass.

Yet, I have to admit, I used to think it was all fun and games myself.

My Story

Raised in a conservative Christian home, I grew up loving Halloween. We had the perfect neighborhood for trick or treat and I always came home with a bag heavy with candy. There was never a question about whether it was a good idea to celebrate Halloween. In fact, most churches threw parties and mine was no different. We dressed in creepy costumes and watched such inspiring fare as "Drink the Blood of Dracula."

Back before costumes were available in every store I created my own, scrounging through closets or sewing my own original designs. In high school, I made a charcoal cape lined with black, slicked back my hair, and wore heavy Dracula makeup to school. I enjoyed the appreciative stares as I swooshed dramatically down the hall.

I went on to attend a Christian college where our school proudly sponsored a haunted house. Bloody victims lurked behind doors; ghosts and ghouls jumped out from every corner to the delight of all.

My love for dress up fun didn't end with my own childhood either. When our first daughter was old enough to take trick or treating, I dressed her up as Dorothy in the Wizard of Oz, complete with glittery red shoes. When she was five, I designed a cardboard cutout with the lyrics of "I'm a little teapot" printed on the front. The cardboard "lid" was secured to a beanie. We practiced the song and motions with her at home until she had it down to a "tea."

I even made costumes for my parents to wear to our Sunday school Halloween party. We dressed Dad up as a punk rocker with spiked hair and a studded wristband. For Mom, I created a giant apple costume out of an old red bedspread, which we stuffed with newspaper. For her head, I made a hat with a stem on top that tied under her chin. My husband went as a farmer in striped coveralls. I made a leopard costume for myself out of animal print fabric, complete with tail and ears. We had great fun, before and during the party, admiring everyone else's costumes.

However, my appreciation for Halloween came to a crashing halt in 1992. The pastor of our church invited all adults to meet in the gym and watch the movie, *Halloween: Trick or Treat*. We were all horrified to learn the history and *current practices* of what we had viewed as a harmless holiday. The evil going on behind our happy escapades challenged my husband and me to rethink Halloween. How could we, as committed Christians, participate in something we now knew to be a grand tool of Satan?

Jeremiah Films interviewed a number of church leaders, law officials, former occult members, and currently practicing witches. They also showed actual footage of cult worship that chilled me to the bone. Those saved from the occult feel pretty strongly when asked what they think about believers celebrating Halloween.

Former Satanist Glenn Hobbs said: "It makes me sick...Christians should be the ones who are standing up *against* this. There are people out there who don't just celebrate Halloween with Trick or Treat candy. This is a religious holiday to them. This is something holy and sacred, and they are taking innocent human life. I can't say, 'go ahead and have Halloween fun'...because Satanists are using this as a smokescreen."

I began to do my own research and everything I read convinced me Halloween is in direct opposition to all Christ came to save us from.

Most holidays in America are faith-based or celebrate qualities valued by the Christian worldview. Thanksgiving, Christmas, New Years, Easter, Valentine's, Presidents' Day, Memorial Day, Labor Day, Mother's Day, Father's Day, and Fourth of July honor godly principles. They have been set aside to honor our parents, express gratitude, delight in love, rejoice in freedom, and most of all, celebrate the birth and resurrection of Christ.

Just what do we celebrate at Halloween? Do we honor God by our participation, or spread the Good News about Christ through it? It's time to open our eyes and look beyond the fuzzy eared toddler costumes and bags of candy.

Author and former Satanist Bill Schnoebelen says,

"Today a revival of the practices of Druidism, along with various forms of witchcraft are sweeping Europe and North America. While occult procedures and their rituals may vary in intensity, the fact is that witches, as well as Satanists commemorate Halloween night with the same fervent dedication to invoke spirits for personal power."

Chapter Three: How Halloween Began

Pastor Doug Warwick of Calvary Chapel writes: "Halloween can be traced back to the ancient religious practices of the pagan Celtics in Ireland and northern Britain. The main feast day in their religion was at the end of summer, when they believed the physical world and the spiritual world were at their closest point of interaction. Because the division between worlds was so thin at that time, according to their belief, evil spirits easily 'made the jump' into the physical world, rising out of their graves and wandering the countryside in search of their physical homes.

"During this festival of the dead, the Celtic priests, called Druids, performed religious rituals of animal, and sometimes human, sacrifices to appease their over 300 gods and to ward off the evil spirits. The bones of the sacrifices were piled with wood and set ablaze. This "bone fire" (now known as a "bonfire") represented the sun and was believed to frighten away evil spirits." (*from "Annual Thoughts of Halloween" by Doug Warwick, 2013).*

http://www.nuggetnetreview.com/m-should-i.htm

The Halloween symbols used today were not picked at random. Halloween glorifies witchcraft and demonic power. All its imagery comes from the occult:

- Witches practice magic and call forth spirits in order to gain personal power. The black cloak is a reminder that Halloween is a 'festival of the dead.'
- Broomsticks are a phallic symbol (representing the male organ) believed to transfer orgasmic energy into spiritual power.
- Jack-o-lanterns represent damned souls; the candle inside, the fires of Hell. Turnips were originally used in Europe. Many set out jack-o-Lanterns to show spirits they were sympathetic to their plight, in order to avoid being tricked.
- Bats were feared by the Celtics who believed they communicated with the dead.
- Black cats are familiar spirits or magic helpers, an evil soul with supposed powers, or witches in disguise.
- Skeletons represent death and the afterlife of the unrepentant.

Tarot cards, horoscopes, séances, Ouija boards, fortune telling, palm reading, and black and white magic are just a few forms of witchcraft practiced today. God hates them all. Why? He hates them because they lure mankind - which He created - whom He loves and sacrificed His one and only Son to save - into dependence on the power of Satan. They may seem like games at first, party entertainment, or harmless diversions. That's exactly what Satan would have us think.

He knows how to deceive people into believing they're not doing anything wrong, even though God clearly tells us in the Bible that it's wrong. "The acts of the sinful nature are obvious: sexual immorality, impurity and debauchery; **idolatry and witchcraft**...I warn you, as I did before, that those who live like this will not inherit the kingdom of God" (Gal. 5:19-21, *NIV*).

Before Halloween existed, Manasseh, King of Judah, got into trouble for practicing these things. He could have been a good king. He had God's Law and His power available to resist temptation. Instead, "He **sacrificed his sons** in the fire in the Valley of Ben Hinnom, practiced **sorcery, divination** and **witchcraft**, and **consulted mediums and spiritists**.

He did much evil in the eyes of the LORD, provoking him to anger" (2 Chron. 33:6, *NIV,* author's emphasis).

God hasn't changed His mind even though Halloween comes brightly packaged and candy wrapped.

Paul's words to the Thessalonians warn us to stay alert to these dangers, even when they're disguised. "Abstain from evil [shrink from it and keep aloof from it] in whatever form or whatever kind it may be" (1 Thess. 5:22, *Amp.*).

This might seem far-removed from the Halloween of today. We have "safe" parties at churches and schools where children can show off their costumes, play games, and eat treats assured to be drug and razor blade free. Stores and malls open their doors to welcome trick or treaters during daylight hours, accompanied by moms, dads, and family members. We ooh and ahh over how cute they look and post their pictures on Facebook to show all our friends. What could be wrong with such an innocent day of fun?

Chapter Four: Halloween Today

In the most quoted chapter of the Bible, king David wrote, "I will fear no evil, for you are with me; your rod and your staff they comfort me." (Psa. 23:4) Yet, at Halloween, Christians not only do fear evil, they revel in it! They delight in the latest thriller, tell scary stories, visit haunted houses, and dress as gruesome characters.

I was shocked and saddened by the costumes I saw on the kids in our youth group when I walked in on their party. My sweet friend came running up to greet me, her face blackened, "blood" dripping from her eyes and "wounds" on her face. "I'm a zombie!" she gleefully announced. She gave me a quick hug and scampered away. Sadly, I remembered my own Dracula getup.

I recalled another church party where I watched *Drink the Blood of Dracula*. We were thrilled to be scared out of our wits. It inspired me to create my own Dracula costume. However, the vivid images from that one movie produced nightmares that haunted me for years. It doesn't look like we're doing any better as a Church now. Even though we offer optional activities and Harvest Parties, the "Event" is still Halloween and the kids know it. We're still sending the message that "fear is fun and harmless."

"What is Halloween? It is a celebration of evil born out of pagan superstitions. It is a demon-inspired festival of death. It is the high holy day in the Satanic Church, the day Satan is glorified. On Halloween, witches and Wicca observe satanic rituals, cast spells to oppose churches and individual Christians, and offer blood sacrifices to Satan." (*Pastor Doug Warwick*)

My first awareness of this kind of activity by the enemy came from my pastor, H.B. London, Jr. He had just returned from a speaking engagement and told us about his experience on the plane. The well dressed woman seated next to him refused the meal, saying she was fasting. He assumed she must be a Christian.

"What are you fasting for?" he asked.

"Oh, I worship Satan" she said, and we have a list of leading pastors and evangelists in America we're praying and fasting against."

He gulped. "Do you have the list with you?"

"Yes," she said, showing it to him. He noted many friends and colleagues on the list, as well as his own name.

"Thank you," he said, handing it back. He didn't bother to introduce himself.

The enemy is very serious about targeting Christians for destruction. Why do we think we can play near the fires of hell and not get burned? We don't have to look far to see proof of the growing intensity of Halloween in our society.

Halloween is Not Just Harmless Fun

Look at the entertainment offered every fall. Movies year round are becoming darker, and Halloween is the embodiment of everything evil. Blood thirsty characters exude wickedness; evil is portrayed as powerful and inescapable. Our heroes have changed as well. They're no longer men and women with moral principles and courage, taking a stand for truth and justice. They're drunkards, thieves, curvaceous vamps, not to mention vampires, and werewolves.

We pay money to watch their exploits, and their values are becoming the values of our society. We applaud them when they win. They are the teen idols of this generation and heart throb of young girls!

The recent fairy tale remakes actually mock the virtues they were originally written to teach. And television offers a vast array of thrillers and series glorifying witchcraft, demonic activity, and monstrous acts of violence. Commercials horrify and tantalize the young, innocent, and vulnerable at every station break.

The games children play on laptops and tablets are increasingly violent as well. Death is no longer a shocking occurrence to be mourned, but the intended outcome of each game. Our kids participate in death and dismemberment in full color with realistic sound effects to enhance the experience. And we wonder why angry youths resort to killing their schoolmates, teachers, and family members.

Look at the products being sold. The "Dead Dog" rejected by horrified Sears, Wal-Mart, and Amazon shoppers is only one example of what's available for Halloween. Specialty stores are springing up everywhere to cater to America's lust for the grotesque, trying to outdo one another with their costumes, decorations, and haunted houses.

Look at the news. Halloween-related crimes, gory remains of sacrificed animals, and an increase of occult symbolism surface each year. Hal Lindsey, author and American evangelist says, "We have found all over the country, reports of animals that have been mutilated in a very skillful and specific style that shows that they have been used as sacrifices. There have now been confirmed cases where girls have been used as breeders, and their infant children sacrificed to Satan....Halloween is the time when all across the country, in secret little places, in the dark, there will be little babies sacrificed to Satan."

They believe if you kill an animal, it releases energy they can exploit for Satan's purposes, especially on their high holy day of the year – Halloween.

It's not just happening in big cities where you might expect violence and Satan worship to flourish. My husband worked fourteen years as a volunteer policeman in our city of 4,500 in the late 80's and early 90's. Every year during September and October they found evidence of occult ceremonies and animal remains in the woods and on beaches.

My girlfriend lives in a quaint little town on the coast fifteen minutes from here. In October 2013, she and her teenage daughter were coming back from a beach walk when they passed a group of women in a circle, wearing capes of various colors. They looked like a happy group, but my friend thought the capes were kind of unusual.

They were surrounded by symbols, some made with rocks and others drawn in the sand. They appeared to be preparing for some sort of ceremony. When they got home her daughter looked them up - *all* were symbols of the occult. These normal looking women chatting on the beach were Wiccans performing a ceremony in full view of passersby, in the middle of the day!

Finally, look what former Satanists say – those who have been redeemed from witchcraft, demon possession, and fear. "I was a generational Satanist...my earliest rememberings of Halloween and some of the things that were involved was that it was a very dark time for me. It was something that I didn't enjoy." (*Glenn Hobbs*)

He goes on to tell about his participation in a human sacrifice - a little girl named Becky. One of the women in the coven had been impregnated with this child to sacrifice on Halloween. She and Glenn were put together in a shack and abused repeatedly throughout the month. On Halloween night they put them both in a van and drove to where the ceremony had already begun. They took Becky and left him in the van.

"I could hear a lot of commotion that was going on. People were screaming and yelling, and a low murmuring was going on. So I knew in my mind that there was some type of ritual going on, because I'd heard it before." After a while, a woman came to get Glenn and led him to a stone altar. He didn't know their intentions at first.

"They could have just been sacrificing an animal over her, or it could have been a sexual abuse from the high priest onto her."

The little girl's feet were spread apart and her arms and legs tied down. She was ghostly white. He saw they had slit the bottoms of her feet and wrists and were passing around chalices of her blood for people to drink. "Then the high priest took the athame, or the ritual knife, and he picked it up and he put my hand on it and then he forced it into her chest."

"This is something that happens every Halloween. There are children all over the world who are losing their lives, during Halloween night. And as a society we celebrate it, and we go door to door and ask for candy and it's a big celebration to us. It's quite ironic how one group of people are thinking it's fun and another group of people are taking human life. And yet there's this wall, and no one seems to want to face the facts of what's really going on." (*Glenn Hobbs, Halloween: Trick or Treat?*)

We may feel like our children are insulated in our homes against this kind of wickedness, but unless we teach them a clear difference between what is good and what is evil, they can easily succumb to the temptations around them.

Carol Matricianna, co-host of *Halloween: Trick or Treat?* explains: "By understanding the origins of Halloween, we can no longer claim ignorance. As parents, we're called to a sense of responsibility and must decide whether or not to allow our children to participate in the cultic celebrations which glorify the powers of darkness."

But I Don't Do Any of that Stuff

This is the excuse I often hear from Christians who continue to celebrate Halloween, even after they hear the facts. They don't do any of that bad stuff. They don't worship Satan and don't dress up as anything scary. They go to church sponsored parties where everybody dresses up as Bible characters. It's a lame excuse for mimicking the culture around us instead of being a light in the darkness.

Why don't the rules we use to effect change in other areas apply to Halloween?

- Christians often boycott companies who produce porn or carry products that lead people into other sins. They aren't buying the products in question, but reason that if they can withdraw their financial support in other areas, it will hurt these companies and effectively get their message across to bring change.
- Most Christians do not promote abortion, and therefore do not wear pro-abortion t-shirts or carry pro-abortion signs even if they look cool. Instead, they vote against abortion, volunteer in crisis pregnancy centers to counsel young mothers, who are alone and afraid. And they work to promote family values in our country.
- Many Christians believe it's against God's plan to drink to excess, smoke, take drugs, or gamble. Therefore they don't spend their money in bars, advertise cigarettes, hang out at drug parties, or support the local casino. Instead, they try to treat their bodies as God's

temple. They encourage the addicted to come to God for help. Programs like Celebrate Recovery flourish because they offer hope, and satisfy the craving for God which addictive behaviors cannot.

- Most Christian women don't advertise what's not for sale. They choose to stay pure until marriage and remain faithful to their husbands. Most dress in a way that doesn't tantalize men around them. Instead, they keep their sexy underwear and lingerie for their husband's eyes only.

So why do we stay far from evil - even work to fight against it, and warn our children of the heartache they will experience if they do these things – yet say it's okay to celebrate a holiday that *directly opposes* Christianity and what God loves?

Our Children Are Targeted

What seems like innocent fun is actually early training for our children to accept Satan's traps as harmless. Chuck Smith, co-narrator of *Halloween, Trick of Treat?* says, "One of the biggest promoters of Halloween is the public school system. School sponsored Halloween themed activities often include dances, costume contests, carnivals and arts and crafts projects. Education officials admit that more effort is usually put into the celebration of Halloween than any other holiday, including Christmas and Easter."

At the next level, occult members actively recruit teens. Unless our children are trained to recognize the difference between truth and deceptive philosophies, they can be easily taken in. Maureen Davies, occult researcher says, "We know that this has been going on for many years, this is not new. But their arrogance and their outrightness about the way they recruit is becoming unbelievable."

Sex and drug parties are another avenue occult members use to introduce teens to their beliefs and practices. Dave Hunt, author, speaker and expert on Eastern mysticism and occultism points out the connection, "Since the 1950's and 60's millions of young people in the Western world have been initiated into sorcery. In the New Testament the Greek word for 'sorcery' is 'Pharmakia.' A sorcerer is a person who takes consciousness altering drugs in order to contact spirit beings to gain supernatural powers."

I've often heard addicts and former drug-users talk about how 'spiritual' their experiences seemed when they were high or drunk. In the psychedelic swirl of altered consciousness, Satan's philosophy sounded profound and meaningful. It is a strong deception.

Unfortunately, the adults seeking to lure our kids into this web don't necessarily look like Satanists - wearing all black, pierced, and tattooed. Dave Hunt goes on to say, "The book of Revelation seems to indicate that in the last days, sorcery would be revived. Remember that the drug user today is the University Professor, the doctor, lawyer, psychologist, leading politician. We're being fed the sorcerer's philosophy from the top down."

Bill Schnoebelen, author and former Satanist adds, "The real Satanists, the hard core Satanists, are involved in criminal activity, and for that reason they are going to try and look as normal as possible. They're doctors, they're lawyers, they're teachers, they're oftentimes people who are in positions of great influence over small children."

So how in the world can we protect our children? Who can we tell them to trust? Who can *we* trust? Our first source must be God's Word.

Chapter Five: Comparing Halloween Themes to Scripture

Why do we, who call ourselves followers of Jesus Christ, continue to participate in a holiday that celebrates death, fear, darkness, and witchcraft? Is this what the Bible teaches? What Jesus taught? He promised us better things. We need to learn what God's Word says to make wise decisions for our family and future generations.

This is what scripture says about the seven most prominent themes of Halloween (all scripture is taken from the *NIV* unless otherwise noted).

Death

The most obvious theme of Halloween is death. Jesus said He came to give us life – eternal, abundant, and free. He calls us to choose life, not death.

- "This day I call the heavens and the earth as witnesses against you that I have set before you life and death, blessings and curses. Now choose life, so that you and your children may live" (Deut. 30:19).
- "For those who find me find life and receive favor from the LORD. But those who fail to find

me harm themselves; all who hate me love death" (Prov. 8:35-36).

- "Since the children have flesh and blood, he too shared in their humanity so that by his death he might break the power of him who holds the power of death—that is, the devil—and free those who all their lives were held in slavery by their fear of death" (Heb. 2:14-15).

See also: Psa.16:11; Isa. 25:7-9; Ezek.18:32; John 10:10; 1 Cor. 15:55-57

Fear

The world claims it's fun to be afraid, to fill up on thrillers (the more shocking the better), and get frightened out of your wits at haunted houses. This sends the message to our kids that it's all pretend – the spirit world isn't real. Yet, the Bible gives a completely different message. God calls us to choose faith in Him rather than fear of man or demonic power.

- "Don't be afraid," the prophet answered. 'Those who are with us are more than those who are with them'" (2 Ki. 6:16).
- Whoever dwells in the shelter of the Most High will rest in the shadow of the Almighty. I will say of the LORD, 'He is my refuge and my fortress, my God, in whom I trust'...He will cover you with his feathers, and under his wings you will find refuge; his faithfulness will be your shield and rampart. You will not fear the terror of night, nor the arrow that flies by day, nor the pestilence that stalks in the darkness, nor the plague that destroys at midday" (Psa. 91:1-2, 4-6).
- "This is what the LORD says: 'Do not learn the ways of the nations or be terrified by signs in the heavens, though the nations are terrified by them. For the practices of the peoples are worthless....Do not fear them; they can do no harm nor can they do any good.' No one is like you, LORD; you are great, and your name is mighty in power" (Jer. 10:1-3, 5-6).
- "Submit yourselves therefore to God. Resist the devil, and he will flee from you. Draw near to God, and he will draw near to you. Cleanse

your hands, you sinners, and purify your hearts, you double-minded" (James 4:7-8, ESV).

See also: Psa. 23:4; 27:1; 34:4, 9 and 11-14; 46:1-3; Isa. 41:10; Rom. 8:15

Darkness

Satan is the opposite of God in every way. If Jesus came that we might have light, Satan comes to make us prisoners of darkness. He doesn't want us to see and know the truth about Jesus. God calls us to abide in and share His light.

- "And this is the judgment: the light has come into the world, and people loved the darkness rather than the light because their works were evil. For everyone who does wicked things hates the light and does not come to the light, lest his works should be exposed. But whoever does what is true comes to the light, so that it may be clearly seen that his works have been carried out in God" (John 3:19, *ESV*).
- "The hour has come for you to wake up from your slumber, because our salvation is nearer now than when we first believed. The night is

nearly over; the day is almost here. So let us put aside the deeds of darkness and put on the armor of light" (Rom. 13:11-12).

- "For you were once darkness, but now you are light in the Lord. Live as children of light....Have nothing to do with the fruitless deeds of darkness, but rather expose them. It is shameful even to mention what the disobedient do in secret. But everything exposed by the light becomes visible—and everything that is illuminated becomes a light....Be very careful, then, how you live—not as unwise but as wise, making the most of every opportunity, because the days are evil" (Eph. 5:8-17).

See also: Isa. 5:20; Matt. 4:16; 1 Pet. 2:9; 1 John 1:5-7

The Occult

References to spells, incantations, demonic power, and dark forces abound in the month of October. Halloween movies and thrillers portray the enemy as powerful, and he is, but his power is restricted. Only God is omniscient, omnipresent, and omnipotent (all-knowing, everywhere, and all-powerful). God invites us to be filled with the Holy Spirit, rather than fear or seek demonic power.

- "Let no one be found among you who...practices divination or sorcery, interprets omens, engages in witchcraft, or casts spells, or who is a medium or spiritist or who consults the dead. Anyone who does these things is detestable to the LORD, and because of these detestable practices the LORD your God will drive out those nations before you. You must be blameless before the LORD your God" (Deut. 18:10-13).
- "When Jesus had called the Twelve together, he gave them power and authority to drive out all demons and to cure diseases, and he sent them out to proclaim the kingdom of God and to heal the sick" (Luke 9:1-2).
- "You cannot drink the cup of the Lord and the cup of demons. You cannot partake of the table of the Lord and the table of demons. Shall we provoke the Lord to jealousy? Are we stronger than he? 'All things are lawful,' but not all things are helpful. 'All things are lawful,' but not all things build up" (1 Cor. 10:21-23, *ESV*).

- Finally, be strong in the Lord and in the strength of his might. Put on the whole armor of God, that you may be able to stand against the schemes of the devil. For we do not wrestle against flesh and blood, but against the rulers, against the authorities, against the cosmic powers over this present darkness, against the spiritual forces of evil in the heavenly places. Therefore take up the whole armor of God, that you may be able to withstand in the evil day, and having done all, to stand firm" (Eph. 6:10-13, *ESV*).

If you want to read about an exciting demonstration of God's superior power, read 1 Ki. 18:26-39. Other good examples in: Isa. 47:9-14; Eph. 3:16-21 and 5:11-12, *ESV*

Conformity

Our Savior wasn't afraid to stand up for what was right, even if it meant going against the crowd. Jesus was a holy rebel who spoke against the sinful practices of His day. He offered no compromises, preaching only repentance and forgiveness.

Surprisingly, and to the delight of the downtrodden, He was hardest on those already in the house of God.

Paul told his young protégée, Timothy, "God has not given us a spirit of timidity, but a spirit of power, of love, and of self-discipline. So do not be ashamed to testify about our Lord" (2 Tim. 1:7-8, *NIV*). God calls believers to nonconformity – to be unique, set apart for His use – to stand strong, even when we stand alone.

- "Do not conform any longer to the pattern of this world, but be transformed by the renewing of your mind. Then you will be able to test and approve what God's will is—his good, pleasing and perfect will" (Rom. 12:2).
- "Do not be yoked together with unbelievers. For what do righteousness and wickedness have in common? Or what fellowship can light have with darkness?....What agreement is there between the temple of God and idols? For we are the temple of the living God. As God has said: 'I will live with them and walk among them, and I will be their God, and they will be my people.' Therefore, 'Come out from them and be separate,' says the Lord" (2 Cor. 6:14-17).

- "You adulterous people, don't you know that friendship with the world is hatred toward God? Anyone who chooses to be a friend of the world becomes an enemy of God. Or do you think Scripture says without reason that the spirit he caused to live in us envies intensely? But he gives us more grace" (Jas. 4:4-6).
- "Beloved, do not imitate evil but imitate good. Whoever does good is from God; whoever does evil has not seen God" (3 John 1:11, *ESV*).

See also: Rom. 12:9, *ESV*; Col. 2:8; 1 Thess. 5:22, *ESV*; 1Tim. 4:7, *ESV*; 2 Pet. 1:3-6

Greed

Every child who comes to our door Halloween night thrusts his candy bag forward and says, "Trick or Treat!" (i.e."Gimme what I want or I'll be back later to egg your house!")

We respond with a smile and say, "Oh, isn't that cute?" As if it's exactly the kind of manners we want our children to practice. All year long we teach them about Christ who came not to be served, but to serve, and give His life as a ransom for many. Yet, on this night of ghouls and goblins, we suddenly cheer for greed and gluttony. We reward the demand for goodies with an enthusiasm that boggles the mind.

Jesus said, "Watch out! Be on your guard against *all* kinds of greed; a man's life does not consist in the abundance of his possessions" (Luke 12:15, italics added). This command applies to cars, clothes, money, craft supplies, and, yes, even candy. Instead, the Bible encourages us to give to those in need.

- "Let not my heart be drawn to what is evil, to take part in wicked deeds with men who are evildoers; let me not eat of their delicacies" (Psa. 141:4).
- "When you sit to dine with a ruler, note well what is before you, and put a knife to your throat if you are given to gluttony. Do not crave his delicacies, for that food is deceptive" (Prov. 23:1-3).
- "So whether you eat or drink or whatever you do, do it all for the glory of God" (1 Cor. 10:31).

See also: Prov. 25:16; 2 Cor. 8:7; 2 Cor. 9:10-11; Jas. 4:1-4

Childish Fun

Contrary to what the world seems to think, God loves parties. In fact, He *invented* the whole idea. The Old Testament is full of invitations to party, with specifics on how *not* to be a pooper. God said: take a break from work, get together with friends, play music, dance, eat, and give to others. God created us with a need to let down once in a while and have some fun.

That's why He instructed the Israelites to celebrate nine specific feasts throughout the year.* They were special times to be glad and thankful for all God provides.

*The nine Feasts God gave the Israelites are introduced in the books of Exodus, Leviticus, Numbers, Deuteronomy, and Esther including: Passover, Unleavened Bread, Firstfruits, Weeks (Pentecost/Harvest), Trumpets (later called Rosh Hashanah/New Year's Day), Day of Atonement (Yom Kippur), Tabernacles (Booths/Ingathering), Sacred Assembly, and Purim.

There's a big difference, however, between leading our children in God-honoring parties, and allowing them to get sucked into worldly thinking and Satan's definition of fun.

- "Whoever causes one of these little ones who believe in me to sin, it would be better for him to have a great millstone fastened around his neck and to be drowned in the depth of the sea. Woe to the world for temptations to sin! For it is necessary that temptations come, but woe to the one by whom the temptation comes!" (Matt. 18:6-7, *ESV*).
- "Check out everything, and keep only what's good. Throw out anything tainted with evil" (1 Thess. 5:22, *Mess.*).

The question, then, is not whether Halloween is a good idea, but what to do instead. As any recovering addict will tell you, whenever you quit a habit that's been a big part of your life, you need to replace it with something better. Otherwise you'll leave a vacuum that will suck you right back in.

I didn't want to participate in a cover up for evil, but I knew it would be hard to give up the fun associated with Halloween. Our Church Fathers understood our God-given need for fun. That's why they planted Christian holidays on the calendar on the same dates or seasons as existing pagan festivals. This gave God-followers a better focus and helped them channel their energies into holy days that glorified God.

When I found out there was already a Christian holiday November 1st , I knew it could be the perfect thing to replace Halloween. What I didn't know, was how to begin.

Chapter Six: A Better Option

It's no accident that we celebrate so many holidays during the winter months. The ancient Druids feared winter. They believed the sun and harvest wouldn't return, unless they made frantic attempts to appease their gods. So they lit 'bone fires' (defined in chapter three) and performed a series of sacred rituals. Although steeped in fear and superstition, the drinking, dancing, sex, and music were a temptation, even for Christians.

All Saints' Day first came on the scene in the seventh century. Pope Boniface IV introduced an All Saints' Day celebration in May, in order to remember Christians martyred for their faith. Two centuries later Pope Gregory III moved All Saints' Day from May to November to offset the fall pagan festivals. After the Reformation, the Protestant church added this holiday to their calendar also.

By placing Christian holidays on top of pagan festivals, the church fathers hoped Christians would influence people with the message of faith, instead of joining in demon worship. However, superstitions arose around the new holy day. All Hallows' Eve became a night of fear instead of the prelude to a victorious Christian celebration it was intended to be.

Those who were superstitious concluded, if Saints were honored on All Saints' Day, then demons and spirits of the damned must roam the earth the night before in protest, on All Hallows' Eve. If they had to go out on October 31, they would dress up like demons. Perhaps the spirits wouldn't harm them if they could blend in. Others began to put out food to appease any who might be angry and ward off bad luck.

Soon, people lost their fear. Dressing in costume, fortune telling, collecting treats, and Hallows' Eve parties (eventually shortened to 'Halloween') began to gain popularity. When people from the British Isles immigrated to the United States, they brought Halloween with them.

When I tell people I observe All Saints' Day, not Halloween, they often say, "Well that's different." I think that's the *point*. Paul's letter to the Romans says, "Do not conform any longer to the pattern of this world" (Rom. 12:2). At that time Rome was the epitome of indulgence, idol worship, and sexual deviation – a lot like our country today. Refusing to conform to the world around us *is* different, and incredible evidence of the love we have for Christ.

For the past few years, I've worked to educate other Christians about Halloween and All Saints' Day, so they can make an informed decision on how to spend the month of October. We have the opportunity to reclaim this season for God's glory. It's up to us to take back October!

Today, most people in the Protestant church have never even heard of All Saints' Day, and those who have are turned off by some of the strange practices connected with All Saints' Day - somber processions to gravesites, mourning chants, and incense. Those who refer to it as the "Day of the Dead," bring departed loved ones their favorite foods and pray for them (which scripture prohibits), inviting their souls to come visit. Compared to brightly colored Halloween costumes, laughter, music, and food, is it any wonder All Saints' Day lost out? That wasn't the original plan at all.

In his "Annual Thoughts of Halloween," Doug Warwick explains what happened: "Into this pagan culture entered Christianity. Instead of refuting and correcting these pagan practices, the Church *compromised* God's call to holiness by *blending* Christian traditions with the pagan traditions. Pope Boniface IV introduced All Saints' Day to replace the pagan festival of the dead, but without removing any of the practices of the festival of the dead" (author's emphasis).

http://www.nuggetnetreview.com/m-should-i.htm

So the key is not to blend the old with the new, but to celebrate what God loves in ways that carry God's message of truth.

The new holy day was supposed to honor Christian martyrs. More than any other time before in history, our brothers and sisters all over the world are suffering persecution for the Name of Christ – threats, financial ruin, false accusations, torture, imprisonment, and death.

Perhaps we should lead our children in a season of gratitude for their steadfast testimony, instead of going door to door to beg for candy. October can be Christian Heritage month – to learn about true heroes, thank God for them, and pray for Christians around the world. This will prepare us for when we need to take a similar stand.

November 1st is party day – a day of thanks for *all* the saints (which the Bible defines as a believer), whether they were martyred or not. Our Christian ancestors passed on the faith so we could know Jesus today. *That's* something worth celebrating!

We need to offer our kids something better than pseudo-Halloween parties disguised as harvest gatherings, or Bible character dress-up. How creative can you get with that anyway? You wear your bathrobe and tie a towel on your head and you're done. No, we need to get back to the holiday that really means something. How are we going to live today to set an example for the generations to follow? It's time to stop copying the world and be original.

Halloween: A Cheap Imitation

We live in a world of copies. 'Rolex' watches appear on sidewalks at drastically reduced prices. McDonalds serves specialty coffees that mimic Starbucks. Designer look-alikes are available at every department store. You can get non-fat, calorie-free ice cream, beverages, and just about everything else. We buy cheap imitations because we want the look, the taste, and the feel of the real thing, but aren't willing to pay the price to get it. That can be good if you're trying to stay within a budget or lose a few pounds, but in the spiritual world it can be lethal.

God is the Only Original Designer

Satan can't create anything new; all he can do is copy and distort what God has already made. He's out to steal God's customers, so he presents a product that impersonates what God offers. Only his goal is not customer satisfaction. Satan's goal is to completely destroy mankind. One of his most effective weapons is to make us *think* we're getting the real thing when we settle for his cheap imitations.

Instead of participating in his version of fun, why don't we use this season to fight against evil and celebrate what is good? True, it will cost more. Are you willing to pay the price of being different in order to follow Christ?

These verses from Apostle John call us to live in abundance: "Stay with what you heard from the beginning, the original message. Let it sink into your life. If what you heard from the beginning lives deeply in you, you will live deeply in both Son and Father. This is exactly what Christ promised: eternal life, real life!" (1 John 2:24-25, *Mess.*)

Show your Spirit!

We called them Spirit Freaks in college. They wore matching t-shirts, sat down front at every game, and yelled their guts out for our team. They were anything but killjoys. They were animated, enthusiastic, and hoarse by the end of every game. We all knew which team they cheered for, and their spirit was contagious. Their excitement spread to the rest of the fans and encouraged the players.

Some believers are called Jesus Freaks. Filled to overflowing with the Holy Spirit, their life goal is to identify with Jesus Christ, work on the front lines, and be verbal about their faith. They're animated, enthusiastic, and vocal about whose side they're on. Hang out with Jesus Freaks and you can't help but catch their enthusiasm. Their exuberance energizes the team, and revs up the cheering section. You can always recognize a Jesus Freak.

Ask Susan Brooks. She realized she had supernatural powers at a young age. She began dabbling with a Ouija board her mom gave her. The more she participated, the more frightening and violent séances became. She emerged with teeth and claw marks on her arms, marks of strangling around her neck and constant nightmares. Then she encountered true, born again believers.

"I saw in these people a happiness and a joy that couldn't be faked by that many people. And I knew that they had something that I wanted....When they said that something was the person of Jesus Christ I was the first one up there. I knew in my spirit that was the answer, not suicide and not drugs."(from *Revival of Evil* by Liberty Films) Until then, she had planned to step in front of a car and end her life.

Susan discovered the truth that should be evident in each of us – that Christians are different from others because of our love for Jesus Christ. Paul said to "Always be prepared to give an answer to everyone who asks you to give the reason for the hope that you have" (1 Pet. 3:15). If they're not asking, maybe it's because they can't see any difference in us.

Mixed messages can be confusing, exasperating, and sometimes dangerous. My husband has been attacked more than once by dogs who initially greeted him with enthusiasm and a wagging tail. They looked at him with a 'smile'... just before they bit him. I've sat in people's homes who were more interested in interacting with their television than the guests sitting in their family room. I've had people smile pleasantly, look me in the eye, and lie to my face. I don't want to live a life of mixed messages.

We can reclaim October for God's glory with a clear message about who we love and live for. Instead of joining the world's party, we can reclaim this season and make it appealing and meaningful to our families and our churches. This is the light of hope our world needs.

Chapter Seven: All Saints' for Today's Believers

As children return to school, and the weather cools, we turn our thoughts to indoor pursuits. Long summer days are gone and we fill our homes with candles, for their cheerful glow and warm scent. Their fragrance mingles with the aroma of muffins and cookies, priming our tummies for delicious holiday treats to come. Our thoughts turn to gratitude for God, His provision, and shelter. This is a God-honoring holiday season.

In "Why All Saints' Day Matters" Ryan Hamm points out the value of appreciating our Christian roots, and why it's important for modern believers to celebrate this ancient holiday:

"All Saints' Day is a time to remember and celebrate the saints of both past and present. From St. Paul and N.T. Wright to Mother Teresa and John Piper, there is a 'great cloud' of faith heroes to be honored. Beyond these famous names, All Saints' Day is also a time to cherish the universal Church—the rich and poor, old and young, male and female."

Later in the article he points out how warped the holiday became. "There are all sorts of rituals associated with All Saints' Day that might seem superstitious or even, well, weird. But All Saints' Day is a reason to celebrate for all Christians—yes, even you who are perusing a website for twenty- and-thirty-somethings and living in 2011....On All Saints' Day, Christians are also...reminded of the *current* Christians around the world....You've got saints of every nation, every language, every job, every walk of life...all worshipping the same God."

relevantmagazine.com/god/deeper-walk/features/27189-why-all-saints-day-matters

Today's young parents are looking for ways to make their faith viable and encourage godly passion in their children. A modern approach to All Saints' Day is a great way to nourish that. It just needs updating within biblical parameters. The first thing that needs clarification is the definition of a saint.

What is a Saint?
Saints are not just those canonized by the Catholic Church. They don't have to be a martyr or even wear a golden halo. Saints are born again believers who actively pursue intimacy with God and other believers. They're not perfect in living out these goals, but purposefully head in that direction. In other

words, if you've asked Jesus to be the Lord of your life, *you* are a saint.

Vine's Expository Dictionary of Old and New Testament Words says, "Sainthood is not an attainment, it is a state into which God in grace calls men."

The word saint is used sixty-eight times throughout the Old and New Testaments. Here's just a sampling of what it says we can expect to experience. I don't know about you, but reading this list of present blessings and God's future plans for us really excites me.

1. Saints experience God's protection – 1 Sam. 2:9; – Psa. 34:8-10
2. They delight in one another – Psa. 16:3; Eph. 1:15-16; Phi. 4-7
3. They can't help but praise God – Psa. 30:4-5; Psa. 31:23-24; Psa. 149:1, 4-5
4. God stands vigil over the death of the saints – Psa. 116:15
5. They will receive God's kingdom – Dan. 7:18; Eph. 1:18-21
6. The Holy Spirit prays God's will for the saints – Rom. 8:26-27

7. They will be appointed to judge angels – 1 Cor. 6:1-4
8. Saints are called to spiritual warfare through prayer – Eph. 6:10-18; Rev. 5:6-10
9. Saints are the Bride of the Lamb – Rev. 19:6-9

Let's Have Fun!

And now for the part you've been anticipating. Hopefully, you've either been challenged to rethink Halloween, or you've already turned away from what the world has to offer and are looking for something better. You may or may not have known about All Saints' Day, but are open to ideas on how to make the season FUN and meaningful for your family and church.

I would like to suggest a whole season of fun activities for you to choose from. Every October - before summer ends - the world gears up for Halloween. Rather than stand by the sidelines and wring your hands over what your children are seeing and hearing, you can actively pre-empt these messages with Jesus' joy and merriment.

When my husband and I first decided to celebrate All Saints' Day, there was no pattern to follow, so we made up our own. I hope the following party plans and resource lists give you a "starter kit" to work from, as you begin a new adventure. You will find your own style as you go along, and I hope, create new traditions for your children and grandchildren. Let's reclaim this season for Holy Partying!

The rest of this chapter highlights nine keys I've found helpful in a successful launch toward taking back October – decorate, talk up your chosen holiday, get excited about Christian heritage, eat, throw a party, enjoy music, play games, fill the need for dress-up fun, and pray with power and fervency. Chapters eight and nine are full of suggestions on how to accomplish this in your family and church life.

The first thing you always do for any major holiday is:

1. Decorate

Why should All Saints' Day be any different? But the question is – how? I discovered in my research the official colors of All Saints' Day are red - for courage, and white - for faith. If you make fall colors your underlying theme, you can add red and white without looking like you're confused and think it's Valentine's Day. Use leaves, nuts, wreaths, dishes, and candles in fall colors. When October approaches hang red and white banners with scripture in gold lettering on the walls (step by step instructions on how to make your own banners are in **chapter 8**).

The cheerful, inspiring décor of your home will be a refreshing change from the garish black and orange lawn decorations, cobwebs, and skeletons outside. Scripture banners on the walls definitely stand out and make great discussion starters. When people ask about the banners; it gives you an opening to talk about how much fun you're having with All Saints' Day. If your children still live at home, read the verses aloud as you hang each one up. If you have an All Saints' Day party, invite your guests to read them with you.

2. Talk Up Your Chosen Holiday

This is huge. It's important to be bold about what you're doing. If you're excited about All Saints' Day, your children are more likely to see it as delightful too. One year in early October, a cashier asked my daughter the expected questions, "So, are you ready for Halloween? What are you going to dress up as?"

My daughter answered with six-year-old exuberance, "Oh, we don't celebrate Halloween; we celebrate All Saints' Day. We decorate the house for it and have a party and everything. We play games and have a *feast*. And we spend all month reading stories about Christians who did cool stuff!" (That year we were reading about George Washington Carver. She was especially impressed by all the things he invented out of peanuts.)

We immediately had the cashier's attention, as well as the bagger and the lady in the next checkout line. She immediately came to our line to join the conversation. All three pummeled us with questions, which we gladly answered. Our children can be our best ambassadors.

Another opportunity to share appeared when I asked my daughter's first grade teacher if they were planning a Halloween party at school. I explained that we celebrated All Saints' Day instead. She was a Christian and asked if I could tell her a little about it.

She not only listened, but asked if I would write a short description for her to read to the class. They were intrigued. She came up with her own way to honor our beliefs by hanging a "Be a Saint" poster in the classroom that month.

All October long, the children could earn stickers by their name, when she caught them doing and saying nice things for others. They still had a party for Halloween, but a seed was planted for the Christian worldview.

3. Get Excited About Christian Heritage

All Saints' Day was originally set aside to honor Christian martyrs. Thanks to groups like *The Voice of the Martyrs*, and books like *Jesus Freaks* and *The Narrow Road*, we can read about and pray for men, women, and children around the world who face persecution today.

We don't have to limit ourselves to honoring martyrs when celebrating All Saints' Day, however. We can thank God for *all* Christians who have and are currently living wholeheartedly for God. It's exciting to hear their stories and how God has met their needs. They give us examples to follow.

In the introduction to *Who's Who in Christian History* the editors say it well: "We are the inheritors of a tremendous legacy that has been ill-acknowledged. By this neglect we deprive ourselves of a rich benefit. Here are thrilling accounts of courage, adventure, and endurance...men and women who made a lasting impact on Christian faith and experience. They followed 'Jesus, the author and finisher of faith' – and yet 'they, without us, are not complete.' May their inspiring stories encourage us and our generation to run the race as they have run."

For too long, we in the church have deprived ourselves of this. People are starving for heroes today. We don't need to read and watch fictional stories; we already have centuries' worth of examples at our fingertips - true stories about real people overcoming evil and temptation!

An angel held back a pit of hungry lions from devouring Daniel, because he was blameless in God's sight. The Spirit of God plunked Phillip down on the road beside the chariot of an Ethiopian eunuch, who just *happened* to be reading about the Messiah and wondered what it all meant. Lo and behold, here was an interpreter!

Luther rocked the church and started a revolution when he nailed his Ninety-Five Theses to the Wittenberg door. Amy Carmichael rescued hundreds of girls in India from temple prostitution. Joni Eareckson Tada discovered she was freer as a wheelchair bound quadriplegic *with* God, than she'd ever been without Him.

When people live recklessly to bring God glory and share His love, it's exciting and miracles are everywhere. New stories are being lived out every day. Let's get in on some of the blessings God has for us by getting to know our brothers and sisters in the Body of Christ. It's a guaranteed faith booster and worth every moment you invest.

4. Eat

Of course, no holiday is complete without food. It always makes an occasion more exciting and the word "feast" makes it sound like a big occasion. Which it is.

If you decide to host an All Saints' Day party, your "feast" can be as fancy or casual as you like. If you serve dinner, you could offer to make the main course and have your guests bring side dishes. Or you could designate a special menu that's only for All Saints' - like having turkey for Thanksgiving, ham for Easter, or corned beef and cabbage for St. Patrick's. This is a chance to start your own traditions.

If you want to keep it casual and focus more on games and activities, finger foods are perfect. Special treats for movie nights throughout October with your family will sweeten the time, as well as when you're reading biographies or devotionals together. This will build memories to savor for years to come.

5. Throw an All Saints' Day party

Make it the talk of the neighborhood. This is the exciting climax to the season. Dinner, games, and a family friendly movie is a perfect night of fun. Add games to get people up and moving. **Appendix E** has instructions for several we have used or you can make up your own.

6. Don't Forget Music!

Music is an essential part of any celebration. Most hymnals list a few songs under the heading "All Saints' Day," and there are many contemporary songs that are perfect for this season. You can start your own play list especially for the month of October and use it at your All Saints' Day party.

Prompt your kids to listen for songs on Christian radio and at church. Start a list of ones you want to purchase or download. It will inspire you! As you run errands together, see who can be the first to identify lyrics about courage, faith, sacrifice, or being an example for the next generation. Keep score and award the winner!

Another fantastic resource is a compilation of songs by 24 top contemporary artists called "The Story." The beautifully written lyrics are based on a person or group from the Bible, and how their stories intersect with ours. Play them for your family and let them guess who they're about *before* you show them each title.

7. Play Games

Bible trivia games and sword drills are easy and don't take any set up time. There are free Bible apps for your phone as well. Other games that spotlight faith and courage are available from Christian bookstores, homeschool catalogs, and Christian publishers.

8. Fill the Need for Dress-up Fun

Most children love to play dress up – whether in sparkly princess dresses, high heels, and tiaras, or super hero capes, masks, and weapons. I didn't want my girls to miss out on the fun I had creating and wearing costumes of all kinds. So we had costume parties throughout the year for occasions *other than* Halloween.

Drama is a great outlet for dress up fun. Our homeschool group put on plays for family and friends. The kids wore costumes and makeup, sold tickets, and made half-time treats. We rented the youth room at our church and the kids performed to a full audience every time.

My girls and their cousins started their own tradition at family vacation. They decided to dress my youngest daughter as a different character each night after dinner. Their self-imposed rules were they couldn't plan ahead, and had to make the costume out of whatever was in the vacation house. They managed to transform her into an Egyptian princess, Whitney T'nager, a tennis star, a bum, Johnny Appleseed, and a clown. The pictures are priceless, sparkling with laughter and happy memories.

When my youngest daughter and I studied mime, her "final" was to perform with me in full makeup and costume for her grandparents. We had fun choosing what "face" we wanted from pictures at the library, and applied our makeup with nervous giggles. The show was a great success.

9. Pray With Power and Fervency

This is a fun and exciting season, but we also need to be diligent warriors – to break the power of the enemy and rescue those being lured into and harmed by the lord of Halloween. Pray against the evil that seeks to devour our nation. Pray for the innocent born or drawn into the occult, especially those who are tortured and killed as offerings to Satan.

Fight for what is good with the same fervency our enemy uses to fight against us. But don't give in to fear. It's easy to be consumed by thoughts of darkness when learning about these atrocities, so keep your eyes open to the light. Remember, Satan is a defeated foe; he has already lost the war.

A Final Word:

If you're married, make sure your husband or wife is on board with your decision about All Saints' Day before you make plans to include the whole family. If you want to celebrate All Saints' Day, but they're not convinced yet, it can sabotage your enthusiasm, confuse your kids, and divide your home. The best way to win him or her over is to respect their feelings and not push your ideas on them.

Pray for God's Spirit to speak to them, and do what *you* can to celebrate our fabulous Christian heritage on your own. Read the stories of Christian heroes and tell others what you're learning. Talk it up with your kids, and be an example of joy. Celebrate All Saints' with interested friends at a time that doesn't force your mate into a corner or put them in a bad light. Speak well of him or her to others. Hopefully, your enthusiasm will be contagious and your husband or wife will catch the vision and join you.

The same things apply to your church family. Share what you're learning, invite those who show an interest to celebrate with you, and don't criticize those who continue their old habits. A positive example is more engaging than sour-faced criticism.

May God bless you, your household, and your church in this exciting fall season as you love and honor all Jesus came to give us. As you stand boldly for Christ, *"Do not be overcome by evil, but overcome evil with good"* (Romans 12:21).

Chapter Eight: Taking Back October at Home
All Saints' Day Activities for Your Family

Now for details on how you can put these ideas to work in your family life.

1. Decorate

I've already covered the basics of decorating in the previous chapter. I'm sure you will adjust as the years go by according to the ages of your children and personal taste. If you're interested in making your own All Saints' banners, follow the step by step directions below.

How to Make an All Saints' Day Banner:

1. To make two banners you will need: one yard red or white fabric (choose one that's sturdy, such as kettle cloth or upholstery fabric, so it won't droop); gold or silver puff paint for writing the scripture; 4 wooden dowels – ½" wide by 18" long (or 2 – 1 yd. lengths to cut in half); and 2 yards decorative fabric ribbon to span the width of the top and bottom of your banner (I used a white jacquard pattern for our white banners and black and red ribbon

accented with gold for the other); and 1 yd. matching braid or rope to create a hanger.

2. Cut fabric along fold lengthwise to create 2 pieces, 1 yard in length, for your first two banners. Wash and iron.

3. To finish the sides of your banners, turn under ¼" on each side and press. Turn under again 1," and press. Stitch 1/8" from the edge.

4. To make sleeves to slide your dowels through - turn the top and bottom edge under ¼" and press. Turn under another 1," press and stitch 1/8" from the edge.

5. To create the hanger: cut braid into 18" lengths and finish ends by melting or tightly wrapping with scotch tape. Measure 2" in from each side at the top of your banner and pin ends of braid in place on the back. Stitch securely.

6. Cut 2 pieces of decorative ribbon approx. 1" longer than the width of your banner. Pin first ribbon to banner 1" down from the top sleeve and the other 1" up from the bottom sleeve. Wrap extra around to the back for a finished edge, or turn under before stitching. Stitch 1/8" from each edge of the ribbon at the top and bottom of your banner.

7. Now you're ready to add the scripture of your choice. Type the words on a computer; select a font that's easy to read. Use the horizontal orientation on Page Layout, so it will be wide enough for your banner. Enlarge the type enough so that the verse fills the banner's width, with a margin at each side. Arrange printed pages on the banner and make adjustments until you're pleased with the look.

8. Pin the printed papers to your banners with sheets of carbon paper underneath. Carefully trace each letter, pressing hard enough to write on the fabric. Remove papers.

9. Use puff paint to trace letters and let dry for amount of time recommended.

See scripture options for your banners at the end of the book in **Appendix A**.

Your banners should last for years if you store them carefully. I wash mine in cold water and hang them to dry. Iron out wrinkles from the backside, being careful not to overheat the paint and accidentally glue it to your ironing board. To store, lay all banners together with dowels in place, and roll them like a scroll. Store in an under the bed box or tube container.

I pray they will be a joy to your family and inspiration to all who see them. They also make great gifts for friends or family members, who would love to have them, but aren't inclined to make one themselves.

2. Talk Up All Saints' Day

Before you go any further, let your children know you plan to make changes this year. Explain why you want to turn away from Halloween as a family. Keep your focus more on what you *can* do instead of what you're *giving up*. Emphasize All Saints' Day and how much we have to be thankful for in our Christian heritage. If they're old enough, ask them if they can see where the focus of each holiday naturally leads. Moses used a similar method in his "choose life or death" speech to the Israelites in Deuteronomy 30:11-19.

3. Get Excited About Christian History

As the days grow shorter and the weather cooler, it's a perfect time to read with your family. My children loved reading new biographies every October. We learned about some pretty amazing people. Today, there are even more quality books available for every age group.

Of course, the Bible is our first source of inspiration, but God's story is still being written in the lives of His children today. Biographies, missionary books, magazines, and blogs are all good sources for true stories of faith and courage. God's faithfulness never ends.

It's so easy to get busy with things that have no eternal value. So we're forewarned to conscientiously do our job as parents: "Watch yourselves closely so that you do not forget the things your eyes have seen or let them slip from your heart as long as you live. Teach them to your children and to their children after them" (Deut. 4:9).

My faith has been tremendously strengthened by all I've learned about individuals in the 'great cloud of witnesses.' Now that my children are grown, I continue to spend the month of October reading biographies and sharing what I learn with others.

Check your local thrift stores for treasures. I recently bought a bagful of practically new hard covers for less than $5 each. I can't decide which one to read first! For a list of book recommendations - children through adults - see **Appendix B** at the end of the book. You will also find a lesson plan for homeschoolers, "Four of My Favorite Saints" in **Appendix D** that you can modify for the ages of your children.

Movies

Faith-based movies are not only great entertainment, but help us get to know *true* heroes our children can look up to. I especially look for ones which highlight faith and courage. Lately, there's been an exciting surge of quality Christian movies being produced. I encourage you to load up your family and see them in the theater first to show support for these efforts.

When *God's Not Dead* came out, our church filled a bus and drove an hour to watch it as a group. It was like a foretaste of heaven when - four times throughout the movie - the audience broke into spontaneous applause, for characters that stood strong for God, despite personal sacrifice.

For a list of movies you might want to watch, see **Appendix B**. Be sure to check ratings and story descriptions to see whether the movie is appropriate for the ages of your children.

4. Eat

Need I say more? This is covered in chapter seven and I'm confident you can take it from there.

5. Throw a Party

We try to invite a different group of people every year, in order to introduce the concept of All Saints' to as many as we can. For those who know little or nothing about it, it's helpful to give them a short summary of what you're celebrating.

I say something like, "Hey, we're going to have an All Saints' Day party on November 1st and we'd like you to come. We're going to have (a sit down dinner or finger foods) and then play some games and watch (name of movie). All Saints' is a Christian holiday to honor martyrs and great people of faith throughout history. We plan to play games featuring Christian heroes."

Then I give them a chance to ask questions, which usually brings up the topic of Halloween. Depending on their level of interest, I explain why we've chosen All Saints' Day over Halloween and what a positive effect it's had on us spiritually. Even if they're not ready to give up Halloween, they're usually open to learning something new, especially if it comes in party form.

I let them know we're going to focus on people from the Bible and Christian history so they can be prepared. The games are a lot more fun when people have time to think ahead about some of their favorite heroes. Often, people will do a little research and bring a short bio about a lesser known individual and we all have fun getting to know someone new.

6. Don't Forget Music!

Music is an even bigger part of our lives today with so many portable devices available. Even when it's playing in the background and we think our kids are unaware of the lyrics, they pick up more than we realize. How many times have your children suddenly busted out with a jingle from the TV or radio, or songs from church you didn't know they knew? What you listen to is of utmost importance.

Every holiday has special music we associate with it. Why not All Saints'? We have abundant choices. See **Appendix C** at the end of this book for recommendations.

As people arrive on party night, it's nice to have upbeat music playing, as well as during the meal. If any of your guests are musicians, you might ask ahead of time if they'd like to play a couple songs with inspiring lyrics, or accompany the group in a few worship choruses. If you happen to have a fireplace or outdoor fire pit, so much the better!

7. Play Games

Your first game could include music. Play the first 10 seconds of a song to see who can be the first to call out the title. The winner could be the first one to get 5 correct. If you have guests of all ages, be sure to have a mix of old and new songs so everyone has a chance. This makes it even more fun.

Make games as simple or complicated as you want. Adjust the difficulty, length of game, and prizes according to the age and abilities of your guests. It should be fun and interesting for everyone. Look for instructions on how to play: "Who's Who in Christian History," a "Heroes" matching game, and "Do You Know" trivia game in **Appendix E**.

8. Enjoy Dress up Fun for Other Occasions

Once you begin planning creative dress up opportunities, you'll have so much fun you won't want to stop. Your children will remember these special times all their lives, and you'll get the reputation for being the family that knows how to have a good time. Shouldn't Christians have more, good clean fun than anybody?

I hope the following stories will spur some ideas of your own for dress up parties.

When my girls were little, we enjoyed picking themes for each party and letting the guests get creative with their costumes. One birthday party featured candy. My girls dressed as Skittles - one lime green and the other purple. I made giant circles out of fabric with drawstrings at the top and bottom, and holes for their arms. We stuffed them with newspaper to make them round, and they wore tights and tennis shoes.

Their friends arrived as a pack of gum, the candy fairy, a bag of M&Ms, and other assorted treats. We gave a personalized award for every costume (such as sweetest, most creative, sparkliest, longest lasting etc.). They played candy related games, and of course, ate candy.

Then there was the Princess Party featuring a castle my husband and I made from a refrigerator box - with a draw bridge, window, and battlements cut at the top. The girls took turns standing on the stool inside, making up their own lines for an impromptu drama. We planned games and treats accordingly.

The next dress up birthday had a Circus theme. This was the first time they invited boys. Another refrigerator box served as a circus wagon with barred windows to look out of, which we incorporated into one of the games. Their friends came as a circus master, clowns, a bear, an acrobat etc. The parents who were willing also dressed up. As a special treat, we hired a professional clown to give a show. However, in the close quarters of our living room, the kids were too scared of him to enjoy it!

I admit I still love dress up even though my children are grown. Who says grandparents are too old to play? One year for my husband's birthday I threw a "There's only one Kelly Vice" party for him. Before the party, I secretly delivered a life-sized photocopy of his face on card stock to family members. Their job was to make it into a mask or mount it on a stick, and arrive at the party "in disguise." We all posed together for a picture with him in the middle and it always makes us laugh.

When he turned 50, I threw a surprise Hawaii 5-0 party for him, complete with Hawaiian music, food, and décor. Everyone came in luau attire. A Hawaiian family in town catered the meat and the rest of us brought side dishes for a terrific feast.

Now that my oldest daughter is married, she and her husband find creative ways to have dress up fun. They and their friends have had 50's and 60's parties, a Ninja and Super Hero birthday parties. Every year on Christmas morning, she and her husband arrive at his mom's in costume – one year they came as elves, and when their son was born, they all dressed in super hero jammies. Now they have two boys and who knows what will come next.

9. Pray With Power and Fervency

October is ours to claim – to celebrate God's goodness and get to know our heroes, past and present, in the Body of Christ. Part of the joy of the season is seeing God's direct answers to prayer. But we won't be able to enjoy the rewards unless we do the work.

Here are some prayer ideas for you and your family:

1. Praise God for the beauty of the season, for homes to protect us from the cold, and that we have a party-loving God who wants us to rest and play together.

2. Praise God for faithful believers, who were and are, willing to die rather than deny their Savior.

3. Praise God for the worldwide Church - who love the Lord Jesus Christ and want to live faithfully for Him - and for our ancestors who passed down the faith.

4. Pray for those being persecuted around the world - that God will give them protection and deliverance, if He chooses to spare them - or courage, hope, and boldness, if their deaths would more effectively spread the gospel. For details of specific individuals go to the Voice of the Martyr's website.:

http://www.persecution.com/public/newsroom.aspx

Print their stories and fill a bowl at the center of your dinner table. Draw one each day to pray for by name. It's easier to pray when you can see a face, and be aware of the spiritual war around the world. You can also sign up to receive email alerts throughout the year to continue praying.

5. Pray for each member of your family – at school, work, home, and in your community. Ask God to make each of you bold, faithful, cheerful, and loving, even when it means being different from the world.
6. Pray against the evil that seeks to devour our nation. Ask God to bind the powers of darkness and loose the Spirit of light in our country. Pray scripture aloud and personalize it with details of current events.
7. Pray for the innocent lured or born into the occult, and those tortured and killed in the worship of Satan.
8. Consider fasting food or something else in order to focus on prayer. Fight for what is good with the same fervency our enemies use against us. But don't give in to fear. When learning about the occult it's easy to despair over the darkness. Remember, Satan has already lost the war.

May God bless you and your families as you seek to go deeper in His love. I pray whatever ideas you glean from this book inspire new traditions, blessing your family for generations. Don't' be afraid to try new things that might feel uncomfortable at first. Holiness is an oddity in our culture.

Adjust as you go along to fit your family. Keep the joy of the All Saints' season alive and do what you can as the Lord leads. As Nehemiah said to the people when they renewed their commitment to holy partying, "Go and enjoy choice food and sweet drinks, and send some to those who have nothing prepared. This day is holy to our Lord. Do not grieve, for the joy of the LORD is your strength" (Neh. 8:10).

The next step is to share what you're learning with your church family and take back October together as believers in Christ.

Chapter Nine: Taking Back October at Church
All Saints' Activities for Every Age

Even if you're not on the pastoral staff, there's a lot of things you can do to encourage your church family toward a fall *full* of God-honoring fun. If you're a pastor, leader, or Sunday school teacher, you have even more opportunities to get things rolling, and affect your entire community for the Lord.

Change comes slowly and old habits are hard to break, so here are a few ideas to capture the interest and support of your church body:

- Get an early start, presenting optional activities to your pastors, board, children's department, Sunday school class, or church body, so you don't conflict with any plans already in the works.
- Keep it positive and upbeat. Keep the main point the main point - to be a Church that honors God with love and holiness in your community.
- Volunteer to do your part; be specific.
- Give copies of *Taking Back October* to your pastoral staff and ask what they think. Would

they be willing to promote All Saints' Day, or declare October Christian Heritage month at your church?

- Ask if the staff would be willing to encourage every age group to focus on Christian heritage during October, to replace Halloween. Every department head - children's pastor, music minister, youth director, Sunday school and small group leaders, and senior pastor – can brainstorm what they could do to promote All Saints' Day.

How fully you carry out the following plans depends on your role in the church and how open the staff is to embrace All Saints' Day. Start with what you *can* do. Encourage others to join in your delight. Hopefully soon, the celebration of saints will overshadow the popularity of Halloween and become the norm for churches everywhere.

1. Decorate

Your church probably already decorates for fall. Why not add red and white banners in the sanctuary or worship area? Ask your worship pastor to commission skilled seamstresses from your church or community to create large scale banners (10' or more in length). This will arouse curiosity and anticipation of All Saints' Day in your congregation throughout the month of October.

The truly crafty will savor the challenge to make one-of-a-kind originals of lasting beauty, for everyone to enjoy. Make sure they have a budget to work with so they can create quality banners worthy of our God.

Children's Department

Introduce what All Saints' Day is about in the children's department. Let them know that people who love Jesus, love what He loves. Compare scriptures on light, courage, faith, and nonconformity with Halloween themes and let the children draw pictures to illustrate the contrast.

Let the kids make their own All Saints' banners to take home and share with their families what they're learning. Make sure you have a sample banner made ahead of time to show them what theirs will look like.

You will need:
- Pre-cut pieces of red and white butcher paper 1'wide x 2' long

- 1′ long wooden dowels to glue or tape to top of banner
- 1′ long piece of heavy string for hanger at the top
- Scriptures printed on white paper to glue to banners
- Paper or fabric ribbon for decoration
- Gold and silver glitter paint to trace scripture

Instructions for Banners:

Instead of sewing banners, as in chapter eight's instructions, children can roll the banner over the dowel and glue or tape them in place. Hand out pieces of string and help them attach one end to each side of the back to create a hanger. See **Appendix A** for Scriptures to use.

Read the scripture choices and have kids choose the one they want on their banner. Help them glue it to the front. Let them choose pre-cut pieces of ribbon to attach above and below the scripture. If time allows - and the teacher willing - let the children trace the words with glitter paint. Lay them aside to dry until the following week when they can take them home.

Youth

Once you've introduced the positives of All Saints' Day over Halloween, invite the youth group to create their own decorations for the teen room or sanctuary. They could help adults make backdrops, banners, or props to go along with the sermon series for the month. Teens love hands-on projects, when they're convinced it's a worthy cause.

2. Talk Up All Saints' Day

Prepare your congregation well in advance that this year you're going to start something new that includes everyone. Share what you've learned about Halloween and how, as God's people, we're called to be different. Rather than conform to what the world tells us we need to do for fun, invite them to join all the exciting plans in store for every age group during October.

3. Get Excited About Christian Heritage
Children

As soon as school begins, start talking about what it means to be a saint. Read a short story or devotion about a different person each week. Do a series of lessons on All Saints' Day during the month of October. Talk about the importance of faith and courage in the Christian life and feature famous Christians from the past, as well as present day heroes.

Challenge the children to show the same qualities in their lives, perhaps even using the "Be a Saint" idea my daughter's first grade teacher invented.

Watch short movies on Christian heroes, or have a movie night. Ask the kids how they would like to emulate that person in some way. Encourage kids to bring a paragraph about a lesser known Christian hero they've learned about each week. Read each one to the group and award prizes to the ones who bring the most.

Talk about martyrs, and read stories of ancient and modern day martyrs. Ask why a person would be willing to die rather than turn their back on Jesus. Ask them to share times they've been made fun of or pressured to compromise their beliefs. How did it make them feel when they stayed strong? And when they gave in?

Youth

All the ideas for children can be used for youth, only on a deeper level. At this age, they're more familiar with peer pressure, school shootings, and bullies. Google "Christian teen martyrs" to find inspiring stories of teens standing strong for Jesus all over the world, to share with the youth group.

Download a free copy of *Jesus Freaks: A Bible Study for Those Who Refuse to Deny Jesus* by Carol Sallee at:

http://persecution.net/download/freaks.pdf

Use it as a special 14 week study. Better yet, invite students to take turns summarizing that week's chapter and lead the discussion.

Have movie nights and watch true stories of brave heroes of the faith. See list of recommended movies in **Appendix B**.

Adults

If all adult Sunday school and small groups are willing to focus on Christian Heritage during October, it will be easier for others to get on board. Group leaders might choose to highlight stories from the *New Foxe's Book of Christian Martyrs*, or study *Jesus Freaks* with their class. There are also collections of Christian biographies and Bible studies on passing on the faith. Look for the lesson plan in **Appendix D** to use for youth or adult Sunday school. If your church has a bookstore, make sure a variety of good biographies and Bible studies are available for purchase, including *Taking Back October*.

The senior pastor could do a series of messages on courage, persecution, what our ancestors have to teach us, and much more. The music minister can weave a mix of hymns and contemporary music with All Saints' themes to promote gratitude for our heritage and inspire courageous living.

4. Eat

You may not need too much direction in this area. We church goers are famous for potlucks, parties, and sumptuous meals at every gathering. Food and fun just naturally go together.

5. Throw a Party!

Party Ideas for Children and Youth

Your church may want to have a party on October 31 as an outreach to your community. If so, let them see and feel the difference Christ makes.

Remember, Jesus went to parties all the time; He hung out with unbelievers so they could hear the message. But His presence always changed what happened at those parties. People were drawn to His grace - His loving acceptance of who they were. And they were convicted by the truth He spoke - the standards of a holy God. We want to be like Jesus and draw others to Him with grace and truth.

So invite the children in. Make it fun; be creative! Do it differently than the world does. Invite the teens to run games and serve refreshments. Here are some ideas:

- Advertise you're having a Fall-In – challenge kids to come as something having to do with fall – leaves, football, caramel apples, the new school year. Play games using leaves, apples, football, trivia questions, and serve fruit with caramel for dipping.
- Invite the community to an *All Saints' Eve* party instead of Halloween. Plan games, food, prizes, and a movie presentation that introduces your neighbors to Christian heritage in fun and informative ways.

For the kids who come regularly, plan a dress up party earlier in September or October. This can release their creative energy in a more productive direction. Or save the big event for All Saints' Day, to celebrate the climax of the season. Make it a red and white party – encouraging everyone to come as items that are red, white, or a mix of both. Explain again these are the colors for All Saints' and they stand for courage and faith. Or throw a Hero Party - where the kids create masks and costumes and come as famous Christians from the past. Pictures of many are available on the Internet.

Adults

Kids shouldn't be the only ones having fun. Have an All Saints' Day party on November 1st for the entire church. Get those fun-loving adults involved in drama, games, music, food, and prizes to make it an event people will remember and talk about all year long.

6. Don't Forget Music

Music can be a strong instrument for instruction and worship. Song videos with lyrics add to the impact. You can also study secular lyrics which reveal the true intent of the enemy in his war against Christians.

Use music for games when possible. Set up karaoke with lyrics about faith, courage, and sacrifice. Ask teen or adult musicians to lead the group in singing, or perform a few favorites of the season.

Another great resource is the two CD set "The Story." This collection of songs by contemporary artists, tells stories of believers throughout the Bible. Use them on your playlist, or for a guessing game, to identify the subject of the song. Refer to the music recommendations in **Appendix C** for additional ideas.

7. Play Games
Children

Play musical chairs to an upbeat version of "When the Saints Go Marching In," like Kids Songs

http://www.kidsongs.com/lyrics/when-the-saints-go-marching-in.html

or Conner Going's YouTube version of himself as a quartet. It's fun to watch and listen to:

https://www.youtube.com/watch?v=nMSLj3x9DPo

There are many other styles and versions available as well.

Depending on the age and abilities of the children, play Bible trivia, lead sword drills, or have children act out a scene from the Bible or history. Outfit them with the pieces of armor listed in Ephesians 6 (available from Christianbook.com).

http://www.christianbook.com/christian-character-building-costume-new-edition/9834504047/pd/504047?dv=c&en=google-pla&event=PLASHOP&kw=toys-0-20&p=1167941&gclid=CK_GsOnn5sACFRaSfgodknsA_w

Set up a shooting gallery or sand bag toss to knock out the enemies of faith and courage. Make your targets "death," "fear," "darkness," "witchcraft," "conformity," and "greed." See how many they can blast. You could also use these themes in a fishing pond or dunk tank. Have a cake walk or apple stacking contest. Set up a hay bale or corn field maze for children to find their way through. Or plan a hayride through town.

Youth and Adult

Obviously, teens are more energetic in their gaming than most adults. However, many teens enjoy an intellectual challenge, so don't dumb down the games for their sake. Just keep it fun and fast paced and provide ample motivation to win.

Instructions on how to play: "Who's Who in Christian History," "Heroes of the Faith," and "Do You Know?" are in **Appendix E**.

You could also play "Charades" with titles of books and movies about heroes of the faith. For instance, for "End of the Spear:" Act out the motion for movie. The title has four words. First word - the person could point to their bottom, touch the end of their nose or pretend to flip through a book until they reach THE END. Fourth word - they could pretend to hurl a spear. Award a prize for the team who guesses the most correctly.

Another hilarious game for teens or adults is "Truth or Consequences" based on the old game show. See instructions in **Appendix E**.

8. Fill the Need for Dress up Fun

Be sure to read the stories in chapter eight for examples of dress up fun all throughout the year. This is the biggest draw to Halloween for most children and teenagers, so it's important that we provide other opportunities to satisfy this need.

9. Pray Fervently

Prayer and the Word of God are the only offensive weapons we've been given to defeat the power of the enemy. From children on up, we need to be proactive in spiritual warfare in our churches. I've already presented ideas for families in chapter eight. Here are some specifically for church prayer times:

Children

1. Go around the room and ask each child to name one thing he or she is thankful for about fall.
2. Ask each child to thank God for a person they know who loves God and exhibits courage in his/her life.
3. Stand in a circle with the children in your class and have everyone hold hands. Pray for every child by name, and for every person who enters that classroom throughout October. Pray they will feel loved, welcome, and want to know more about Jesus.

4. Say a prayer of thanks for martyrs, past and present - for their bravery to stand for Jesus.
5. Ask a different child each week to draw a name of a persecuted Christian from the Voice of the Martyrs' website:

http://www.persecution.com/public/newsroom.aspx

Pray for his/her protection, comfort, and courage.
6. Pray for your city and community, that Satan will not be able to lure children into witchcraft, séances, and watching scary movies. Ask for God's protection and for His light to shine through you to those who don't believe.

Youth

If your teens are participating in a Bible study such as *Jesus Freaks*, they will be much more aware of ways they can be praying - for your church, community, and individuals living recklessly for Christ. Ask them for prayer requests and encourage them to lead whenever possible.

Further ideas:

1. Give thanks that we have a party-loving God. Praise Him for this season and the opportunity to party in distinctively Christian ways – that honor Him and witness to our community.
2. Praise God for persecuted believers, past and present, who refuse to deny God.
7. Praise God for the worldwide Church of believers. Thank God for past generations.
8. Have teens praise God for someone with great faith who has blessed their life.
9. Pray for those being persecuted around the world - for protection and deliverance, or for a bold witness to spread the gospel.
10. Ask a different teen each week to draw a name from the Voice of the Martyrs:

http://www.persecution.com/public/newsroom.aspx

11. Organize a prayer walk. Have the kids meet at the church and divide into teams of two or three, to walk and pray the streets around the church for an hour. Give them a list of topics and scripture to guide their prayers.

- Ask God to bind the powers of darkness and loose the spirit of light in your community through you.
- Pray this season will be full of joy and gratitude in your city, rather than death and violence; that people will spot Satan's lies and be repulsed by images of evil.
- Pray people will not fear Satan and his power, but trust in God's love and power to save them.
- Lift up innocent children, lured or born into the occult, and those tortured and killed in the worship of Satan. Pray occult members are prevented from harming anyone and come to know Jesus.
- Ask God to give you opportunities to tell people about His love and why you celebrate what He loves.

Adults

This is the time for adults to take the lead. All the ideas listed for families and youth are applicable. Two additional thoughts for adults:

1. Schedule an all-church prayer night for any who would like to come. You can keep the

church open for two hours of drop-in prayer, or have a set program. Here's a possible format:

a. Limit the service to an hour or so and resist the temptation to add a sermon.

b. Introduce each theme from a printed sheet and then release people to pray for that theme. They can sit or kneel at their seats, the altar, in groups, or write their prayers on paper provided.

c. Limit prayer times to 10 minutes before calling people back for the next topic.

d. Give people time to reflect and praise in between, by playing or singing a song or two.

e. Subjects to cover could include:

Safety in the community during the Halloween season

For your church to shine brightly for Jesus Christ

For individuals involved in witchcraft and Satan worship to hear the message of Christ and be set free from Satan's grip!

For believers in your city to stand courageously for Christ when mocked, mistreated, or harmed because of their faith

That unbelievers will see joy in the life of each Christian and hunger to know God

2. Another option for prayer night is to create prayer stations for people to go to, with instructions at each station. You might play soft music in the background to create a contemplative atmosphere. Possible stations:
   a. A cross to nail fears to – anxiety over loved ones, memories of past experiences, of demonic powers, or of being different
   b. Tea lights at the altar - to light in prayer for an individual who needs to know Christ
   c. Print scriptures from chapter five on Halloween themes vs. God's truth for people to meditate on
   d. Journaling station - with lyrics or scripture to respond to on paper.

e. Prayer buddies – have pastors and leaders available to pray with anyone in need

f. Flowers of Faith – have a bucket of flowers available for people to praise God for a Christian they have known or admire

3. Organize prayer walks every day of the last week of October. Have a map of your city available for sign ups. Identify what streets and days each person will prayer walk that week. Give each one a list of ideas. Encourage them to go in teams of two and take turns praying out loud as they walk.

This is the beginning of a new adventure for your church. Each year, as you try new ideas, you will anticipate the fall season with increased excitement. When God's people stand apart from the world with joy and confidence, the world takes notice. May others be drawn to His light through your faithful witness, and holy partying, as you take back October.

Appendix A: Scriptures for All Saints' Banners

- "Generation after generation stands in awe of your work; each one tells stories of your mighty acts. Your beauty and splendor have everyone talking; I compose songs on your wonders. Your marvelous doings are headline news; I could write a book full of the details of your greatness. The fame of your goodness spreads across the country; your righteousness is on everyone's lips" (Psa. 145:4-7, *Message*).
- "Therefore, my dear brothers and sisters, stand firm. Let nothing move you. Always give yourselves fully to the work of the Lord, because you know that your labor in the Lord is not in vain" (1 Cor. 15:58).
- "Be on your guard; stand firm in the faith; be courageous; be strong" (1 Cor. 16:13).
- "Now to him who is able to do immeasurably more than all we ask or imagine, according to his power that is at work within us, to him be glory in the church and in Christ Jesus throughout all generations, for ever and ever! Amen" (Eph. 3:20-21).
- "I eagerly expect and hope that I will in no way be ashamed, but will have sufficient courage so

that now as always Christ will be exalted in my body, whether by life or by death" (Phil. 1:20).

- "Now faith is confidence in what we hope for and assurance about what we do not see. This is what the ancients were commended for...without faith it is impossible to please God, because anyone who comes to him must believe that he exists and that he rewards those who earnestly seek him" (Heb. 11:1-2, 6).
- "I have fought the good fight, I have finished the race, I have kept the faith. Now there is in store for me the crown of righteousness, which the Lord, the righteous Judge, will award to me on that day – and not only to me, but also to all who have longed for his appearing" (2 Tim. 4:7-8).
- "They will walk with me, dressed in white, for they are worthy. He who overcomes will, like them, be dressed in white. I will never blot out his name from the book of life, but will acknowledge his name before my Father and his angels" (Rev. 3:4-5).

Other options: Deut. 32:7; Psa. 89:15-17; Psa. 100; Phil. 1:3; 1 John 5:4-5

Appendix B: Book and Movie Recommendations
Books for Children:

Beggars, Beasts and Easter Fire: Stories of Early Saints by Carol Greene

Christian Heroes Books by Janet and Geoff Benge

Hinds Feet in High Places by Hannah Hurnard (an allegory)

Men of Faith and *Women of Faith* by Bethany House Publishers

Pocahontas: True Princess by Mari Hanes

The Pilgrim's Progress by John Bunyan (an allegory; available in modern English)

The One Year Book of Christian History by E. Michael and Sharon Rusten

Trailblazer books by Bethany House Publishers

For Teens and Adults:

A Chance to Die by Elizabeth Elliot

A Man Called Peter by Catherine Marshall

And the Word Came with Power by Shetler and Purvis

Extreme Devotion by Voice of the Martyrs

Father to Nobody's Children by David Fessenden

For Such a Time as This by Lisa Ryan

For Those Who Dare by John Hudson Tiner

Gifted Hands: The Ben Carson Story by Ben Carson M.D. with Cecil Murphey

Hansi: The Girl Who Loved the Swastika by Maria Anne Hirschmann

Hudson Taylor's Spiritual Secret by Dr. and Mrs. Howard Taylor

In the Presence of My Enemies by Gracia Burnham

Jesus Freaks by dc Talk and the Voice of the Martyrs

Just as I Am by Billy Graham

The Last Dance but Not the Last Song, by Renee Bondi

The Last Jew of Rotterdam by Ernest Cassutto

Left to Tell: Discovering God Amidst the Rwandan Holocaust by Immaculee Ilibagiza

Let's Roll by Lisa Beamer with Ken Abraham

Mercy at Midnight by Lois Hoadley Dick

Mosaic: Pieces of My Life So Far by Amy Grant

Mother Teresa: In My Own Words Compiled by Jose Luis Gonzalez-Balado

My Father, Maker of the Trees: How I Survived the Rwandan Genocide by Eric Irivuzumugabe (audio book read by the author)

The Narrow Road by Brother Andrew with jars of Clay

The New Foxes book of Martyrs by John Foxe

Quiet Strength by Tony Dungy with Nathan Whitaker

Rachel Smiles by Darrell Scott and Steve Rabey
Run Baby Run by Nicky Cruz
The Simple Faith of Mister Rogers by Amy Hollingsworth
The Story of the Trapp Family Singers by Maria Augusta Trapp
Through Gates of Splendor by Elizabeth Elliot
Tramp for the Lord by Corrie ten Boom
Voices of the Faithful, compiled by Kim Davis, series creator Beth Moore
When God Turned Off the Lights by Cecil Murphey

Parent Resources:
The Annals of a Satanist by Frank Alvarez III
Celebrating the Christian Year by Martha Zimmerman
Halloween and Satanism by Phil Phillips and Joan Hake Robie

Movies:
"5 Ways to Kill Fear" Skit Guys
http://skitguys.com/videos
"Amazing Grace" 20th Century Fox Home
"Behind the Sun" Open Doors International
"Beyond the Next Mountain" Global Films

"Beyond the Gates of Splendor" Every Tribe
Entertainment

"Bible Brainstorm" Skit Guys
http://skitguys.com/videos

"Billy: The Early Years of Billy Graham" Phase 4 Films

"The Champion" TBN Productions

"Chariots of Fire" 20th Century Fox

"China Cry" TBN Films

"Courageous" Sherwood Pictures

"The Cross and the Switchblade" Gateway Films and
20th Century Fox

"Don't Waste Your Life" Skit Guys
http://skitguys.com/videos

"The End of the Spear" Jungle Films LLC

"Esther" Trimark

"Facing the Giants" Sherwood Pictures

"Faith Like Potatoes" Affirm Films

"Fireproof" Sherwood Pictures

"Florence Nightingale" CPT Holdings Inc.

"Flywheel" Sherwood Pictures

"Gifted Hands" TNT, Sony Pictures

"God's Not Dead" Pure Flix Entertainment

"God's Outlaw" Grenville Film Productions Ltd.

"The Hiding Place" World Wide Pictures

"Home Run" Samuel Goldwyn Films/Provident Films

"A Full House of Blessing: The Inspiring Story of the Nicklas Family," Franklin Springs Family Media

"The Inn of the Sixth Happiness" 20th Century Fox

"Joan of Arc" 1999, CBS miniseries

"John Hus" Faith for Today

"John Wycliffe: the Morning Star" Gateway Films

"Love Comes Softly" 2003, Hallmark Channel

"Left Behind" Cloud Ten Pictures

"Les Miserables" 1998, Columbia Pictures (fiction)

"Luther" 2003, MGM Home Entertainment, Universal Pictures

"A Man Called Peter" 20th Century Fox

"Narnia" series Walt Disney and Walden Media

"Not Easily Broken" Tri Star Pictures

"Pollyanna" 2003, Masterpiece Theatre (fiction)

"Something the Lord Made" 2004, Madden Productions

"Soul Surfer" Sony Pictures Entertainment

"Though None Go With Me" Alpine Medien Productions, Hallmark Entertainment

"Tribulation" Cloud Ten Pictures

Parent Resources:

"Halloween: Trick or Treat?" Jeremiah Films

"Revival of Evil" Liberty Films

Christian Heroes List:

If you want to find additional books and movies, but aren't sure what names to look for, here are some not previously mentioned:

Kay Arthur
Augustine of Hippo
Evelyn (Granny) Brand
Dr. Paul Brand
Amy Carmichael
George Washington Carver
Fanny Crosby
Elisabeth Elliot
Ruth Bell Graham
C.S. Lewis
Eric Liddell
David Livingstone
Beth Moore
George Müller
John Newton
William Ashley (Billy) Sunday
Charles Swindoll
William Tyndale
Andrew van der Bijl (Brother Andrew)
Ravi Zacharias

Appendix C: Music

All Saints' Hymns:

Your hymnbook may have a different listing, but these are the songs listed in ours under the heading: All Saints' Day:

"Faith of Our Fathers"
"For All the Saints"
"Hallelujah! Amen!"
"Holy God, We Praise Thy Name"
"The Church's One Foundation"

Contemporary Songs of Faith and Courage:

There are so many wonderful recent songs that I had a hard time limiting this list! Here are some of my favorites:

"Bible Story" by Scott Krippayne
"The Blessing" by John Walker
"Build Your Kingdom Here" by Rend Collective Experiment
"Courageous" by Casting Crowns
"Crosses and Crowns" by The Darins
"Faith" by Amy Grant

"Fearless" by dc Talk

"For Future Generations" by 4Him

"God's Not Dead" by Newsboys

"He Carries Those Who Carry the Cross" by The Darins

"Hands and Feet" by Audio Adrenalin

"I Believe" by Seventh Day Slumber

"I Will Follow" by Chris Tomlin

"If I Labor" by Anointed

"I'm Not Ashamed" by Newsboys

"In Not Of" by Avalon

"It's Not Magic" by Rob Baker

"Live With Abandon" by Newsboys

"Not to Us" by Chris Tomlin

"Our God's Alive" by Andy Cherry

"Reason to Celebrate" by Vineyard Music

"Reckless" by Jeremy Camp

"Say the Name" by Rob Baker

"The Story" multiple artists

"VR" by Rob Baker

"Wake" by Hillsong: Young and Free

"We are the Free" by Matt Redman

"When the Chariot Comes" by The Rescues

"Whom Shall I Fear?" (God of Angel Armies) by Chris
    Tomlin

Appendix D: Homeschool or Sunday School Lesson Plan

"Four of My Favorite Saints"

Why is it helpful to learn about Christians from both the Bible and history?

1. According to Rom. 15:4 – their stories give us hope
2. In 1 Cor. 10:11-13 – they examples warn us not to make the same mistakes, or inspire us with their *good* choices
3. Examples in Hebrews 11 – inspire us to have faith
4. 1 Pet. 5:9 – shows us we're not the only ones who face tough situations

Four favorites from Christian history:

Jonathan:

1. Jonathan chose to be a friend, even when it cost him personally: "Saul's son Jonathan went to David at Horesh and helped him find strength in God" (1 Sam. 23:16). It wasn't safe, but he went anyway.
2. He wasn't jealous of David even though he was the rightful heir to the throne, because

he recognized his friend was God's chosen king.

3. He didn't start a war against his father, even though Saul pursued his best friend to murder him. Jonathan didn't even take David supplies. He pointed to God as David's Deliverer. Because of this, after Jonathan died, David was able to strengthen *himself* in God (1 Sam. 30:6).

4. After showing his friendship and commitment to David, Jonathan went back and served his father, the anointed king, even though it meant separation from his best friend and death in battle.

Discussion Question: How can we follow his example and help others find strength in God?

Gideon:

The angel of the LORD greeted Gideon with, "The LORD is with you, mighty warrior"(Jud. 6:12).

1. God picked the least important guy from the smallest clan in Israel and chose him

to lead His people. Even though he lacked confidence, he obeyed God.
2. Gideon took action, even though his first act of bravery was at night.
3. His father - whose idol Gideon had just torn down - saw the power of God at work and spoke up for him.
4. Even when God's battle plan seemed ridiculous, Gideon obeyed and won a huge victory.

Discussion Question: Do you think you're unqualified to lead others? How has God encouraged you to step out?

Amy Carmichael

1. Went to India as a missionary even when her family didn't support her decision and tried to make her feel guilty for "abandoning" them.
2. She loved traveling the hills of India to preach the gospel, but had to quit when orphan girls and former temple prostitutes began showing up on her doorstep.

3. Amy became bedridden after an accident, and used the confinement to counsel her girls, write songs, poems, books, and letters which continue to inspire people today.
4. God encouraged Amy to die to self, rather than insist on her own way. Because she did, He blessed her work beyond anything she could have imagined. (Biography by Elizabeth Elliot titled *A Chance to Die*.)

Discussion Question: Has your family or a close friend ever criticized you for pursuing what you feel God has called you to do? How has God used disappointments in your life to make you even stronger?

C.S. Lewis:
1. He rejected God after attending a strict boy's boarding school where he saw no joy or meaning in the Christian life.
2. Was haunted by nightmares and guilt, he decided there was no God and became an atheist.

3. God kept pursuing him until he gave his life to Christ. He became one of the greatest Christian authors and speakers of all time.
4. Lewis married late in life, only to lose his wife to cancer. This challenged his faith like never before, deepened his intimacy with God, and brought authenticity and warmth to his writing.

Discussion Question: How has harsh treatment from supposed believers affected your view of God? How did He continue to pursue you even when you turned your back on Him? Has tragedy and heartache brought more depth to your relationship with Him?

Appendix E: Games

"Who's Who in Christian History"

Tell your guests to come ready to share about a Christian – they can be from the Bible, Christian history, or a present day believer.

How to play:

Go around the room and let each person tell about their choice. Each one can only be used once. For instance, for my turn I might say: "My person is George Frederic Handel. He was a child prodigy who almost didn't become a composer because his father wanted him to become a lawyer. His most famous work is *The Messiah,* which a lot of churches still perform at Christmastime. He was only five feet tall, had health problems, and never married, but the music he wrote 270 years ago is still popular.

1. The host or hostess will write each name mentioned on strips of masking tape. After everyone has shared he/she will mix them up and stick a name on each person's back.

2. Send everyone around the room to ask yes or no questions and discover whose name is on their back. (For example: Am I in the Bible? Am I a

woman? Did I write music? Did I get put in jail for translating the Bible into the language of the people?)

3. As everyone figures out who they are, they can go to the side to cheer on the rest. The first person to guess correctly gets first prize, then second and third for successive winners.

"Heroes of the Faith"

Can you match the short biographies with the correct hero of the faith? (Answers are listed at the end)

    a. Martin Luther
    b. Amy Carmichael
    c. Billy Graham
    d. George Müeller
    e. Ruth
    f. Cassie Bernall
    g. Jim Elliott
    h. Corrie ten Boom
    i. King David
    j. George Washington Carver

1. _____served as a missionary to the Auca Indians in South America. He and four other men were

murdered by the tribesmen they had spent weeks befriending. Two of the widows stayed to work among the people that murdered their husbands. The first convert was the man who killed ____.

2. A single woman who, together with her sister and father, hid Jews from Hitler's army, in a secret room in their house. They were discovered, captured, and sent to concentration camps. ____ was the only one to make it out alive. She spent the rest of her life writing books and telling others about the love of Christ.

3. ____was a missionary to India for 55 years. The girls she rescued from temple prostitution called her Ama (mother) and learned trades at the Donavheur Fellowship and about Jesus. After an accident ____ spent the last years of her life bedridden. She wrote 35 books, songs, and poetry.

4. ____vowed to become a monk when hit by lightning, but was later excommunicated when he spoke out against the false teachings of the Catholic Church. His real trouble began when ____ nailed the 95 Theses to the door of the Wittenberg Church.

5. ____ grew up on a farm and never showed much interest in school, but when he gave his heart to

Jesus, he became a student of the Word. He spent his days preaching to rocks and stumps and anyone who would listen. In his worldwide crusades, he preached to more people than ever before in history.

6. God called ____ to care for orphans in Europe and he started an orphanage that housed more than 10,000 children over the years. God challenged ____ to rely completely on Him, so he never asked for money, only praying for what they needed. God took care of every need.

7. ____, her sister-in-law, and mother-in-law all became widows in Moab. She moved to Israel as an alien, yet because of her faith in God, loyalty, and hard work, she caught the eye of a respected man of Israel. She is named in the genealogy of Jesus.

8. He had to run for his life when the king tried to murder him. Even when he had the opportunity ____ refused to take revenge. He said that was up to God.

9. ____ was shot by another student from her school for being a Christian. After years of rebellion, she gave herself to the Lord with wholehearted devotion. Her journal entries have inspired many

teens. Books and songs have been written about her short life.

10. As a young boy_____ hungered for knowledge and overcame the circumstances of his birth, poverty, and prejudice to get an education. ____ eventually got a job at Tuskegee Institute. He is famous for his faith and the hundreds of products he made out of peanuts!

Answers: g, h, b, a, c, d, e, i, f, j.

"Do You Know?"

A lot of men are able to identify what year and make a car is simply by the shape of the headlights or a single body detail. Others can rattle off sports statistics. Many people know the latest in the personal life of popular stars and can give a detailed replay of the latest movie or TV episode. But how much do we know about our Christian heritage?

We say Jesus is the most important person in the world to us and we want to share the message of the gospel. Why is it then, when someone mentions Bible reading or Christian history, the room fills with guilt thick enough to slice? If we fill up on car magazines and the latest from Hollywood, but don't know our heroes of the faith, what does that say we really care about?

Take the following quiz and see what you know:

1. Name 3 movie stars.
2. Name 3 recent movies.
3. Who sings the song _____(name a popular song on secular radio)?
4. What is the next line from _____ (quote the first line of the chorus of a popular secular song)?
5. Have you seen the movie *Prince of Egypt*?

6. Have you seen the movie *Pocahontas*?
7. Who plays Jack Sparrow in *Pirates of the Caribbean*?
8. Name one Gold Medal winner from the last Olympics.
9. Name the current quarterback for any football team.
10. Who holds the highest batting average of all time?
11. Name one of today's most popular cars and why people like it.
12. Name or describe a recent American Idol contestant.
13. Name a current politician (besides the president).
14. Who starred in the recent Mission Impossible remakes?
15. Who sang the hit song "Thriller?"
16. Quote John 3:16.
17. Name 3 people from the New Testament.
18. Name 3 people from the Old Testament.
19. Name a detail from the movies *Prince of Egypt* or *Pocahontas* that is *inaccurate* about Moses' or Pocahontas' life.

20. Two men were named Saul in the Bible; how were they different from each other?
21. Why didn't God let Moses enter the Promised Land?
22. Who wrote the "love" chapter in the Bible?
23. Name 2 great Christian men or women from post-biblical history?
24. Give the name and what facts you know about a missionary from history.
25. Name 2 current missionaries.
26. Name one martyr from the past.
27. Name one martyr from the past 10 years.
28. Name 3 well-known Christians today - not including Billy Graham.
29. Give the title of a book about a Christian hero.
30. Who wrote the book of James in the Bible?

To score - give yourself 1 point for correct answers to numbers 1-15, and 3 points for every correct answer to questions 16-30. Award a prize for the highest score.

"Truth or Consequences"

You will need 3 contestants (all claiming to be *the real* individual in question), a game show host, and an audience prompter to hold up signs for – "applaud," "murmur," and "gasp."

You can provide contestants with a script, or just tell them which one is the real Christian hero and which two are imposters. Then let them come up with their own responses. This can be a scream if your contestants get into role play.

Here's an example for how it might work. Say Eric Liddell is the person in question:

Game Show Host: Would each of you stand and state your name.

Contestants rise one at a time and say, "My name is Eric Liddell," each one trying to sound convincing (they might use an accent or hand motions for emphasis).

Game Show Host: What is the name of the movie that made your story famous to the world? (correct answers are underlined)

Possible responses: "Head Back and Knees High," "The Wind Beneath My Wings," "Chariots of Fire," "Fire Runner," "I Ran Them Off Their Feet."

Game Show Host: What decision did you make during the Olympics of 1924 that shocked the world?
Possible responses: "I refused to carry my country's flag." "I decided I wanted to swim instead of run in the Olympics." "I snuck my girlfriend on the boat." <u>"I refused to run on Sunday."</u> "I got drunk the night before."

Game Show Host: What did you do after the Olympics were over?
Possible responses: "I coached rugby at the University of Scotland." "I became a pastor." <u>"I went to China as a missionary."</u> "I ran for office and made it illegal to play sports on Sunday."

When the questions are done, have each contestant repeat, "My name is Eric Liddell" and the audience cheer for the one they think is the real one. Contestants should jockey a bit, each moving as if he's going to stand up, then finally the real Eric Liddell will rise. Prompter will encourage wild audience applause.

Other Books by Beth Vice Available from Amazon @
http://www.amazon.com

iLove Devotions
The Four Gifts of Christmas
Moments for Homeschool Moms
Peace Within Your Borders: Devotions for
Homeschool Moms

Follow Beth's blog, *Epiphany*.
www.bethvice.blogspot.com
Or write to her @ **jer3113@hotmail.com**

Photo by Sela Photography
http://www.selaphotography.com

Made in the USA
San Bernardino, CA
19 September 2015